Painted By Prejudice:The Thomas Allen Story

C.H.Bordelon

Copyright © 2014 C.H.Bordelon
All rights reserved.
ISBN:0692222383
ISBN-13:978-0692222386

DEDICATION

We would like to dedicate this book to all of those who have served our Nation.

"Darkness cannot drive out darkness; only light can do that. Hate cannot drive out hate; only love can do that."--- Martin Luther King Jr.

WARNING

This book contains material and subject matter that may not be suitable for everyone. Strong racial language and violence are used throughout this book.

ACKNOWLEDGMENTS

This book wouldn't have been possible without the courage and sacrifices of so many great Americans of our past.

Painted By Prejudice:The Thomas Allen Story

Prologue

The early 1900's were a different time and place in the southern half of the United States. Although, slavery officially ended many years ago nearly all of the southern states didn't seem to get the memo. It was long roads, hard work and tough times to be black in this era. Although, they we're supposedly free there were still many things blacks were not allowed to do in the southern states and Mississippi was one of the worst for blacks to reside in.

In 1907, the 29th day of January, a negro baby girl was born on a plantation in Mississippi. Her father worked in the fields on the plantation and her 14 year old mother was a housemaid. This particular plantation's owner would give all the house maids new names, that seemed more suitable to entertain their white guests. It's unclear what the baby's mother's real name was, but the whites called her Ashley so that's the name she lived by. The only name anyone has ever known for the baby's father was Biggin. He was a large man with the hands of a giant. Although his strong hands were useful for some matters, they weren't built for picking cotton. Therefore, Biggins' sole purpose in the fields was to be used as a mule, transporting heavy loads day in and day out. At the ripe age of only 25, Biggins' body was far beyond his years. Due to carrying these heavy loads since the age of 15, his knees and back were not as strong as they once were.

Ashley decided to name her daughter Hannah against Biggins' approval. Biggins felt like any child of his should have a stronger name, a name that would strike fear into anyone saying it. He liked the name Sophia. But after holding his beautiful baby girl in his arms for the first time he realized that something this precious was not meant to be feared, so Hannah it was.

Over the next seven years, Hannah has grown into a beautiful young girl with the voice of an angel. She would sing for hours while picking cotton in the fields and many of the other plantation workers would gather around just to hear her sing soothing melodies. It didn't take long for the plantation owner's wife to hear word about an angel singing in the fields. The owner's wife was a sweet young lady by the name of Meredith. She always tried to treat the workers with respect, without crossing the divided line of black and white of course. Tears fell from her eyes the first time she heard Hannah sing and from that day on, she knew that a voice like this didn't belong in a field. Shortly after hearing Hannah sing for the first time, Meredith convinced her husband into allowing Hannah to sing as entertainment for their guests.

By the age of 14 Hannah has sung so many of the white people's songs that she can barely remember the songs she used to sing in the fields, that filled her soul with joy. Although, grateful she is no longer getting blisters on her fingers in the undying summer heat, Hannah is no longer happy. The amazing sounds that used to vibrate from her body with such ease now have to be forced out. She feels as if there is no longer a reason to sing. Until she met him. He was a 15 year old servant boy of a white couple visiting the plantation. Hannah new from the minute she looked at him that she had to see him again. The angel inside of her has been awakened and she sang like she never sang before, "Sweet melody, I sing to the...oh...oh...sweet melody, I sing to the...we just want to live and be free," the words of her song echo throughout the grand dining hall. The white couple was blown away and insisted that Meredith host a gathering so that everyone could hear Hannah's voice.

Over the next several weeks the white couple returned to the plantation with their servant boy Elijah. It turns out that Elijah has some hidden talents of his own. He can play the piano like a seasoned pro, without ever once having a lesson. Meredith and the couple decide to combine Hannah's voice with Elijah's piano skills. The outcome was truly a match made in heaven.

Meredith and the couple plan a grand ball. Which means in order to be the sole entertainment for a ball of this magnitude, Hannah and Elijah will have to spend many hours practicing their routine. It is decided that Elijah will be staying at the plantation until after the grand ball.

Over the next 3 weeks, news of this grand ball spread like a wildfire and the list of attendees grew longer with each passing day. Hannah and Elijah's feelings for one another also began to grow stronger as the time passed by.

Painted By Prejudice: The Thomas Allen Story

Chapter 1

Hannah and Elijah have now been practicing for three months and the date for the Grand Ball is now only a week away. For the past month, Hannah and Elijah haven't been doing very much practicing at all. In fact, they have been using they're practicing time to explore one another's bodies in ways that neither one have ever done before. After discovering the sensation of sex, they are now madly in love with each other.

Together Hannah and Elijah came up with a plan to run away, to live together forever and be completely free. On the night of the Grand Ball, the guests began to arrive in record numbers. The guests ranged from other plantation owners, small business owners, doctors, lawyers, political figures and the richest people from all around Mississippi. Meredith couldn't have been happier as the guest danced, drank the finest wine and ate like kings. Everything was going according to plan until it was time for the evenings main entertainment, the real reason everyone was here, the chance to hear an angel sing.

With no signs of Hannah or Elijah anywhere on the plantation, Meredith began to get concerned. Her first thought was that one of her rich guests offered to pay them more than she could afford. But then she found Ashley sobbing heavily with a note in her hands. "What's the matter Ashley?" Meredith asked.

But, Ashley could only reply by continuing to sob while handing the note to Meredith. The note read:

I'm sorry ma, it's time for me to move on and live my own life. I didn't mean for this to happen, but I fell in love. He is the angel that makes me sing and I am his fingers that play the keys. Together we are one so goodbye.

Meredith was fueled by anger as she slapped Ashley across the face.

"This is your fault! I knew I never should have taken that little nigger girl out of the fields!"

"I's sorry mama."

"I don't want your apologies, tell me what I'm supposed to tell all of my guests."

"I...I...," Ashley begins to say before Meredith interrupted her.

"Oh never mind, it's not like you're

smart enough to come up with something anyway. Just stop your crying and get back to work.

The guests were outraged after being informed of Hannah and Elijah's betrayal. Meredith heard rude and obscene chatter amongst the guests as they were leaving. "What is this country coming to, when white can no longer control their niggers? It's an outrage, I tell you! It's a pure outrage!"

It has been nearly two years since Hannah and Elijah ran away. They started a life of their own, and left their past behind. Hannah is now pregnant and she is nearing the end of her pregnancy. Hannah has always dreamed of being an educated young woman. But blacks getting an education is still highly frowned upon in today's society. Everyday she tells Elijah how, one day, her baby will change the way the world thinks. One evening, while sitting on the porch of their one bedroom shack, which is remotely located deep in the Mississippi woodlands, Hannah and Elijah discuss names for the baby.

"If it's a girl, we will name her Cheyenne and if it's a boy, he will carry my name," Elijah says, as he slowly rocks back and forth on a homemade wooden rocking chair.

"No, I want my baby to have a white name," Hannah replies, as she rubs her hands across her belly. "What in the world are you talking about woman?" Elijah replies, with confusion in his eyes.

"If it's a girl, she will be called Meredith and if it's a boy, we will call him Thomas Allen."

"You done lost your mind! Why on earth would we give this child a white name?"

"I believe the baby is a boy and Thomas Allen will be a well-educated man that will change the way the world looks at Negros."

"If we give this child a white name, the only kind of life it will ever have is a hard one. It's hard enough to be black in Mississippi without having a white mans name. And the only kind of education we get is a third-rate Negro diploma from the damn fields."

"You learned how to read and write, so why can't our child?" Hannah replies, with anger in her voice.

"You think I'm educated just because I can read and write a little? Let me tell you something Hannah, the only reason they

taught me how to read and write was so I
didn't look so stupid in front of all their
cracker friends."

"You still learned, didn't you?"

"They only taught me what they
wanted me to know. Don't you get it? They
don't want us to be smart."

"And why is that?" Hannah replies.

"Because if we got smarter than them,
what the hell would we need 'em for?"

"I don't know, but I do know that my
baby will have a white man's education. You
hear me Elijah?" Hannah says as she grabs
her stomach.

"What's wrong?" Elijah asks.

"Nothin', I'm...," she begins to reply,
before shouting out in pain.

"What's the matter?" Elijah says as he
jumps out of the chair.

"The baby is ready. Thomas Allen is
on his way!"

Since they never actually bought their
freedom Hannah and Elijah are still
considered slaves so they never leave their
secluded area in the woods, they just simply
live off of the land. With the white peoples
hospitals and going into town to find a
qualified negro out of the question, Elijah is
going to deliver the baby on his own. After

all, how hard can it be, open your legs and push right?

The white couple Elijah worked for, as a servant boy, not only allowed him to read and obtain an education, they actually taught him how to write as well. As a young boy, after learning how to read, Elijah would often read any book he could get his hands on. Somewhere around the age of 13, he came across a medical journal which described childbirth. Still not qualified nor is he experienced, Elijah does however, know a little more than the average person.

"Elijah...he's coming, the baby is coming," Hannah shouts, through agonizing contractions, which seem to be 2 minutes apart from one another.

"Alright...calm down. I'm right here," Elijah replies, as he gently lies her down on the porch.

With every contraction, Hannah's body tightens and the old rotted wood beneath her creeks. Not knowing how to comfort her, when Elijah hears the sound of the creaking wood he passes a joke.

"Now woman, don't go tearing down the house before the baby gets to see it."

Elijah's joke briefly eases the tension

and Hannah begins to smile. A few weeks ago, Elijah made the five mile hike and snuck into town. Aided by the cover of the night, he broke into the doctor's office and stole a small leather medical pouch. It was a simple kit, which included a sharp scalpel, a pair of medical scissors and a few other miscellaneous items.

Armed with his stolen medical kit and mediocre knowledge he gained from reading the medical journal years ago, Elijah is now ready to birth his child. With no sedatives or medication available, Elijah prepares Hannah with the next best thing. He spots a small limb that has broken off of a nearby tree. Elijah put the limb across his knee and snaps it in half. He repeats the process once again and now the limb is only about a foot long.

"Here...bite down on this," Elijah says, as he hands Hannah the broken limb.

With the smile no longer on her face, Hannah reluctantly complies. With the time between each contraction getting shorter and the passageway opening wider, the tiny head of the baby begins to crown.

"You're doing good...keep pushin'," Elijah says, in a subtle attempt to comfort Hannah.

Exactly seven hours later, a beautiful baby boy is delivered by the hands of his father on the 7th day of June 1925.

Chapter 2

With limited medical knowledge and equipment, Elijah was able to successfully deliver his own son, on the rickety porch of their shack, deep in the woods of Mississippi. However, Elijah has no former knowledge of the potential complications of childbirth. Nowhere in the medical journal, that he had once read as a child, did he read anything about internal bleeding.

Over the next few days, Hannah and Elijah continued their discussion about what to name their son. Although, she is not feeling very well and has been put on bed rest by her doctor, Elijah, Hannah can still put up quite the argument.

"He will have a white man's name and get the same education any white man would.

I'll see to that, even if it's the last thing I ever do," she says, with a stern voice while looking directly into Elijah's eyes.

Elijah begins to chuckle as he replies, "Alright...alright, settle down now. Just get some rest and we will talk about it in the morning."

"Uh huh," Hannah replies, as she mumbles under her breath.

Little did they know, this will be the last conversation they would ever have together. Hannah has been suffering from hemorrhages, which means that she's bleeding on the inside. So, tonight when she rests her eyes, it will be for the last time.

The next morning, after awaking to Hannah's lifeless body laying next to him in bed, Elijah spends the next hour cradling her body close to his own. Her face that was once so full of joy and laughter, now only looks like a shadow on the wall, empty and soulless. And her hair that she loved to braid while singing her sweet melodies, no longer shines like it once did before. Now it is only dull and soaked with the tears falling from Elijah's face. After realizing what he must now do, Elijah gathers himself and spends the next several hours digging a grave for the woman he so truly loved. It was a short, but sweet, variation of a funeral. There were only two attendees, a crying, motherless baby and the shell of a man that just lost his soul and reason to live, or so he thought.

For the first couple of days, Elijah could barely look at his son, much less think about giving it a name. He wasn't completely heartless, he did however, manage to find time to feed the baby in-between chores. It takes a lot of time and hard work to live off the land. There's the garden of corn, herbs, spices and peppers, which Hannah usually tended to. And then there's the well, which needs to be pumped daily, the chickens which produced the eggs for breakfast, there's hunting that needs to be done, wood to be chopped and the goats that need to be milked daily, which the baby seems to be quite fond of. All in all, the chores around the house are enough to keep any man busy all day,. mix that with a newborn baby and now you're cooking some gumbo. Just throw a bunch of things into a pot, let it simmer and before you know it, you have a miracle in your bowl.

Three months later, Elijah is still struggling with his pot of gumbo. He is still having difficulties trying to manage his time between the baby and the chores. Although, he no longer refers to the baby as it, he still hasn't given the child a name. But late one afternoon after his chores are through, Elijah is feeding the baby some fresh goat milk. While holding the baby in his arms, the two lock eyes for the first time. He doesn't know if it's the fact that he can literally see the pure innocent soul through the baby's eyes or if it was the smile, whatever it was, something melted his heart. A heart that only months ago was no longer there. Elijah slowly begins to rock the baby in his arms. Moments later, the baby's eyes began to blink slower and slower, until finally he is asleep.

"You got your mama's smile, Thomas Allen," Elijah whispers, as he gently kisses the baby's forehead.

Even through death, Hannah still has a way of getting her point across. She ultimately won the argument of what to name the child and Elijah has also sworn to do everything in his power to give Thomas Allen a proper education.

Another six months pass by and Thomas Allen is now nine months old. He's a beautiful, healthy baby that has just learned how to take his first few steps. Although, Elijah is still slightly struggling with the chores and Thomas Allen, he is significantly better at it by now. But at nine months old, Thomas Allen is no longer satisfied by just lying around in a crib. Elijah notices his sons progression and curiosity of the world beyond the crib.

To keep a closer eye on Thomas Allen, he constructs a frame out of twigs, branches and rope. He then takes one of his old shirts, lines it with cotton and then stuffs it at the bottom, as though to make a mattress. Next he finds four castor wheels, that have been lying around the land, and tightly secures them to the bottom of the frame. "Now then, lets just give this a try," Elijah says to himself out loud, as he places Thomas Allen in the mobile crib. With Thomas Allen's eyes barely breaching the railings, trying to watch every move his father makes, Elijah gets started on his chores. When he is done with one chore and ready to move on to the next, he just simply grabs a hold of the crib and pulls it behind him, this mobile crib idea is working better than even he himself had imagined. Now that he is able to keep a close eye on Thomas Allen, while at the same time doing all the chores that need to be done, the days seem too flow incredibly smoother and faster.

Chapter 3

Now at the age of five, Thomas Allen has been learning how to read and write for nearly two years. Elijah has quickly noticed that his son is an extremely fast learner, but what's even more impressive is his drive to do so. Thomas Allen has also learned how to do some of the chores, which has lightened the load on Elijah. Even though Thomas Allen only does a few of the easier tasks such as spreading feed for the chickens and collecting their eggs, it saves Elijah a great amount of time each day, which is extra time that is well spent. Each night, for exactly one and a half hours, Elijah sits down with his son and teaches him new words. Every Saturday right after lunch at exactly noon, Elijah quizzes Thomas Allen on the words that he has learned throughout the week. And every Saturday Elijah is mesmerized by how well his son performs.

Elijah knew that someday, the day would come when Thomas Allen would start asking the tough questions...the ones that would be hard to answer. But he had hoped that it wasn't at the age of five.

"Papa why in the books are there lots of people?" Thomas Allen asks, in his soft gentle voice.

"Well son...that's complicated," Elijah tries to brush the question off.

"What does comp...comp...complated mean," Thomas Allen replies, as he struggles with the unknown word.

Elijah can't help but laugh. With a giant smile on his face, he does his best to answer the question for his son. "It means hard. Kinda like when you try to pick up two eggs with one hand, but your hands are too small so one always falls."

"Oh, yeah."

"Do you understand what it means now?" Elijah asks, as he raises one eyebrow and looks at his son.

"Yes, sir I do."

"Alright then, you better remember it...it might be on your test come Saturday."

Even though Elijah loves his son with all of his heart, after all, Thomas Allen is all he has left of his sweet Hannah, he also runs a strict household. Elijah knows that in order for his son to rise above the odds in life, he will have to have structure and discipline...

and plenty of it.

In life there are many rules that need to be followed, as well as many consequences if those rules are broken. But under Elijah's roof there's only one consequence for all the many different rules. If any rule is broken, no matter how big or small, there will be one lashing across the back for every year of age.

"I know you're still young, but you know the difference between right and wrong," Elijah says, as he sits his son down for a talk.

"Yes sir."

"From this point on, if you do anything you're not supposed to do or if you don't do the things you are supposed to do, then you will pay the price."

"Yes sir."

The next few weeks roll by without any trouble at all. And then one day, while chopping wood, Elijah hears Thomas Allen laughing. He follows the sound of laughter to the chicken coop, where he sees his son tossing eggs into the air. Every time one of them hits the ground and shatters, Thomas Allen begins laughing. Elijah has seen enough, but instead of tearing into his son right then and there, he goes back to continue chopping his wood. A few minutes later, Elijah calls out for his son, "Thomas Allen, come here boy."

Shortly after, Thomas Allen comes running up from the direction of the chicken coop.

"Yes papa," he says.

"Did you get those eggs collected yet."

"Yes sir, but I...I broke some."

"You broke some, how did you do that?"

"I don't know...they fell," Thomas Allen replies, as he avoids eye contact with his father.

"Mmm...hmm, that sounds strange. You wouldn't be lying to me, now would you boy?"

"No sir!"

Elijah takes a deep breath and slowly exhales as he began shaking his head. "Alright son, go inside and take your shirt off. I'll be there shortly."

Nervous, scared and not quite sure what to expect, Thomas Allen begins to cry as he mumbles, "Ye...yes sir."

Elijah's heart is broken, he can't stand to see his boy in fear of him, but at the same time he knows he has to teach him a lesson. Elijah picks up a thin metal wire that he uses to tie the stacks of wood to one another and enters the house.

Elijah stands in front of his son as he holds the metal wire in his hand. "Go on and get your shirt off now," Elijah demands.

"Yes sir," Thomas Allen replies, with tears streaming down his face.

"You going to get five lashings one for every year of your age. Do you know why you're being punished?"

Elijah calmly asks, "Cuz I broke the eggs?"

"And because you lied about it. That kinda stuff will not be tolerated in this house, you understand me boy?"

"Yes sir."

Elijah raises his hand and then brings the metal wire down across Thomas Allen's back. The wire makes an eerie whistling sound as it rips through the air. When it's all said and done, Thomas Allen has five welts across his back.

Over the next several years, Thomas Allen has lived and learned by the strict hand of his father. At the tender age of only 10, he has become quite the worker. In fact, Thomas Allen handles most of the chores around the house nowadays. But, even more importantly, he has become an even better student and is trying to fulfill his mother's dying wish. There is only a total of three books in the household. All of which Thomas Allen has memorized cover to cover, page by page.

His favorite of the three has a leather book cover on which most of the book's title is no longer legible. Many of the pages beyond the cover are either partially torn, covered in what seems to be blood stains or simply missing completely. Although, this book has clearly seen its better days, Thomas Allen somehow feels as though he is drawn to it, like it had been written just for him. He doesn't know if it's the fact that it is full of magical stories about different trials and tribulations or if it's the hidden messages found far beneath the written words. What he does know is how it makes him feel inside every time he reads from the book. It's the feeling of love, compassion, fear and hatred all rolled into one satisfying feeling of self-purpose.

Thomas Allen has no clue what mystical powers this book may or may not have, he only knows that "ol ible" must be the most profound words ever written in a collection called a book.

It wasn't until a year later, at the age of eleven, that Thomas Allen found out what the real title for his favorite book actually is. Since the age of five, when he really started learning how to read he had always called the book "ol ible." Throughout the years, his father never corrected him either, because he himself didn't know any better or he didn't care enough about a book's true title. Whatever the case may be, Thomas Allen will never forget the first day his father sent him into town alone.

The bright sun had just breached the top of the treeline on a Tuesday morning.

"I'm gonna need you to go to town. Do you remember the way?" Elijah says.

"Yes sir."

"Alright, gather half a basket of eggs, two chickens and five bundles of wood and put them in the wagon."

By "wagon," he really means a homemade two wheeled cart with too long handles used as leverage to lift the wagons stand just above ground level. The rusted wheels of the wagon squeak with every hard turn, which makes it difficult to pull empty, let alone full of wood.

Although, only eleven years old, Thomas Allen has taken after his grandfather Biggin. At his young age, he already stands well above five feet tall, with well-developed

muscles from all the hours that he spends
working the land.

"Now, when you get to town, look for
a sign that says, *Trade Post*," Elijah says.

"Yes sir."

"Ask for Elroy and tell him you my
boy, because he won't remember you."

Thomas Allen has only been into town
with his father three times throughout his
eleven years.

"Yes sir, then what?" Thomas Allen
replies.

"Give him everything in the wagon
and he'll know what to give you. Go straight
there and come straight back home without
talking to anyone else, hear me boy?" Elijah
demands, with a stern manner to his voice.

"Yes sir."

"Well hurry up...you're burning
daylight," Elijah says as he waves his hand
towards the door in a shooing motion.

After gathering everything his father
demanded and loading them into the wagon,
Thomas Allen is now ready to embark on his
journey. Although, Thomas Allen is
undoubtedly strong enough to easily drag the
wagon behind him, he struggles with keeping
it balanced down the long, narrow path
through the woods. The path is littered with

holes, limbs and old tree stumps. After nearly rolling the wagon over ten separate times and five grueling hours, Thomas Allen has finally made it out of the woods and into town.

Thomas Allen eye's are captivated by every storefront, sound and person that he passes on the street. Although, he had been to town before, he had never taken the time to realize that the world has so much more to offer than the life he lives on the secluded land at home. It's nearly 11 a.m. by the time that Thomas Allen finds the sign that reads *Trade Post*.

"I'm looking for Elroy," Thomas Allen says, as he strolls up to the trade post.

"Dat right?" the large, black man standing behind the makeshift table replies.

"Yes, sir. I'm Elijah's boy," Thomas Allen softly replies.

"You sho is gettin' big," the large man replies, with a deep, almost growling, sound of a voice.

Thomas Allen thinks that the man must have swallowed a bullfrog and is trying to talk with it still lodged in his throat.

"Are you Elroy?" Thomas Allen politely asks.

"Dat be me," the large man replies.

"Papa told me to give you these things

and that you would know what to give me in return."

Elroy holds one finger in the air as though to tell Thomas Allen to wait, in which Thomas Allen does. A few minutes later Elroy returns with a large sack draped across his shoulder. He drops the sack on the table and says, "Put da eggs and chickens on the table and put dat wood right here," as he points to the ground next to the table.

Thomas Allen does as Elroy says and a few moments later Elroy returns again. This time Elroy has a large bucket of nails, a hammer and a handsaw, which he places on the table next to the large sack. "Gettcha things and go on home," Elroy says.

Thomas Allen grabs the hammer, bucket of nails and hand saw and then loads them into the wagon. But when he attempts to grab the large sack he struggles to even slightly move it. Elroy finds this amusing and lets out a deep rumble of laughter. The sound of Elroy's laughter reminds Thomas Allen of a late afternoon thunderstorm. He doesn't know why, but suddenly he feels the deep overwhelming urge to join in. Thomas Allen lets out a hearty laughter of his own. Although it's nothing like the sound of thunder rolling off of the clouds like Elroy's, it was a good laugh and it felt great. Thomas Allen then tries to remember a time where he and his papa had ever laughed this hard together. But he couldn't even remember one time that he has seen his father laugh.

After catching their breath from their laughter, Elroy grabs a hold of the large sack and places it in the wagon. "Now go on," Elroy says. Without exchanging another word, Thomas Allen lifts the handles on the wagon and begins to head home.

Chapter 4

As Thomas Allen makes his way
out of town, pulling the wagon down the street, he hears a voice shouting familiar words. "God sent his only begotten son to die on the cross," the unknown voice shouts. As Thomas Allen approaches closer to the voice, he hears even more familiar words, "Jesus died on the cross for your sins." Thomas Allen is now close enough to see the strangely pale -looking man that's shouting the words from his favorite book. "The word is truth and the message is real, it's all right here in the good book," the pale man shouts as he holds a book high above his head. Thomas Allen moves even closer, to see that the title written on the book reads *Holy Bible* not "ol ible" like his. Curiosity gets the best of Thomas Allen, for one because he's never seen anyone with skin this pale and second he wants to know how this man knows

words from his book. *Go straight there and come straight home. Don't talk to anyone,* Thomas Allen hears the voice of his father echo in his head. *But Papa's not here, how would he know?* Thomas Allen thinks to himself.

"We are all God's children," Thomas Allen says to the pale man.

"Not you, nigger! Now get home before school lets out and you find yourself a lot of trouble," the pale man replies.

Hearing the word 'trouble', Thomas Allen decides that the man is right, it's time for him to leave. After all, he wasn't supposed to talk to anyone anyway. Shortly after walking away from the man, he hears a ringing coming from a building less than a hundred feet in front of him. Suddenly the door on the building flies open and a crowd of more pale skinned people rush out and into the street. Thomas Allen had never seen a white person, before seeing the pale man shouting Bible scriptures. So when he sees the crowd of white children rushing out of the school building, his curiosity is raging inside of him. *Who are they? Why do they look like that? Are they sick?* The questions randomly float in and out of his thoughts. Unfortunately, at least one of his questions are about to be answered. Some of the children have spotted him and are now running in his direction. Since life in the woods have a different set of rules, Thomas Allen has no idea that those are not children running towards him...they're trouble.

Thomas Allen and the small group of white children finally cross paths in the street. The small group consists of three boys and two girls, all of which seem to be the same age as Thomas Allen.

"He sure is big," one of the girls says.

"How old are you?" one of the boys asks, while slightly looking up at Thomas Allen.

"Just turned eleven," Thomas Allen says, with a smile.

"Don't you smile at me, nigger!" the boy replies.

"What's your name?" one of the other boys asks.

"Thomas Allen."

All five of the white children begin to laugh.

"Did you...did you say Thomas Allen?" the boy that asked his age replied, through his laughter.

"Yes, that's my name," Thomas Allen replies, as he tries to join them in their laughter. But the laughter felt empty, not hearty like it did with Elroy.

"Well my name is...well my name is Thomas Anthony. I guess that means we're brothers," the boy replies, as he and the other white children laugh even harder.

"I best be getting home now," Thomas Allen says, as he lifts the handles on the wagon.

Thomas Anthony places the palm of his hand hard against Thomas Allen's chest and says, "Hold on... did you say he could leave?" he asks one of the other kids.

"Nope," the other boy says.

"Well, I didn't say you could leave," Thomas Anthony says.

At this moment Elroy turns the corner onto the street.

"Here comes his daddy, let's get out of here!" one of the girls' shouts.

All five of them scatter, but Thomas Anthony turns to shout one last thing, "This ain't over white nigger!" And he was right, it was far from over.

Thomas Allen lifts the handles of the wagon once again and passes by Elroy without a word and quickly scampers out of town. On the long journey home, he can't help but think of two things... his favorite book, in which he now knows is called the Holy Bible, and the word nigger. He doesn't know why, but he doesn't particularly like this word. Until now, he had never heard the word and yet today he heard it three times. He tries to remember a time when his father taught him the word, but he can't remember one. He then thinks that maybe the kids just made it up, but that can't be true, because the pale man with the book said it as well. *So, why hasn't Papa taught me this word?* Thomas Allen thinks to himself. Thomas Allen finally arrives back at home. His father is sitting on the porch awaiting his arrival.

"How everything go?" Elijah asks.

"Good, papa."

"Get washed up, bacon and eggs on the table," Elijah says.

Thomas Allen washes his hands and face in the small, metal wash tub while Elijah empties the wagon. Elijah places the hammer, bucket of nails and the hand saw on the front porch and then carries the large sack inside.

"What's in da sack, papa?" Thomas Allen asks.

"Nevermind boy...jus eat."

Thomas Allen finishes his food

without so much as leaving a crumb behind. Elijah acknowledges his sons unusual appetite, "Hard work going to town, ain't it?"

"Yes sir," Thomas Allen replies, as he lets out a deep breath and rubs his now swollen tummy.

Elijah cracks a slight smile and replies, "Go on to bed, we got a long day tomorrow."

Thomas Allen goes to bed and falls fast asleep without hesitation.

The next morning, Thomas Allen is still asleep in bed when the warm morning sun rays touch his face. Thomas Allen opens his eyes to see his father standing above him, "Bout that time," Elijah says.

"Yes sir," Thomas Allen replies, as he quickly scampers out of bed.

After washing up and eating a couple pieces of bacon, he then meets his father on the porch.

"Bring some water round and then feed the chickens," Elijah says, as he struggles with trying to open the large sack.

Before Thomas Allen has a chance to reply, the top of the sack finally tears open, releasing a thick white powder into the air. The powder covers Elijah's face. Without thinking, Thomas Allen blurts, "Papa, you look like the pale man in town."

Suddenly, from somewhere deep down inside, a rolling thunderish sound explodes out of Elijah. The two share a bonding time of laughter together, which seemed to last a lifetime, but in reality only lasted a few minutes.

After regaining his breath, Elijah says, "They is called, 'white people'."

"Why are they white and we ain't?" Thomas Allen asks.

"Jus the way it is. We was born this way and they was born that way. But don't trouble your mind about that," Elijah replies.

"Papa, what is nigger?"

Elijah's calm demeanor suddenly changes as he feels the blood beneath his skin boiling. "Where did you hear that word?" Elijah asks.

"I heard the pale...I mean the white man, in town, say it. And there was a white boy that said it."

"I told you not to talk to anyone," Elijah says, as he lowers and shakes his head.

This is what Elijah had been worried about all along. He knew that one day he would have this talk with his son, just not so soon.

"Boy, you got painted," Elijah says.

"Painted? Painted...by what?" Thomas Allen curiously replies.

"Prejudice...you got painted by prejudice," Elijah says.

"I don't understand, papa."

"You will...like I said, don't trouble your mind about it right now."

And that was the end of that conversation.

Chapter 5

Another five years have quickly passed by and Thomas Allen is now 16 years old, not yet considered a man, but yet no longer a child. Over the past five years, Elijah has explained Hannah's dying wishes to his son, which Thomas Allen took very seriously. With the age of a blooming young man, and the physical stature of a large full-grown one, Thomas Allen is now six foot two and a half inches tall and weighs a staggering 283 pounds, of pure muscle. Unbeknownst to his father, Thomas Allen has been making weekly trips into town, in the middle of the night. Thomas Allen's sole purpose for his late night visits, is books.

Two years ago, Elijah sent Thomas Allen into town on a supply run. But what Elijah didn't know was that particular day was the grand opening of a new fancy book store, right in the center of town. Thomas Allen's heart began to flutter, his stomach twists into knots with his eyes popping out of his head, the very moment he first saw it. *Just think of all the education in that place,* he thought to himself. Later that night was the first of Thomas Allen's weekly visits.

From the time that he was 14, until now, Thomas Allen has read nearly 50 books, covering many different subject matters. With the knowledge that he has gained from the pages within those books, Thomas Allen now has a much greater appreciation and understanding of the world in which he lives.

Elijah sent Thomas Allen on a supply run earlier today, where a new book release captured his eyes. He knew, without a doubt, that later that night he would be coming back to read this book. But, what he didn't know is how that single decision, would alter his life, for years to come. Thomas Allen returned from his supply run, washed up, ate supper and then waited for his father to turn in for the night.

Elijah has been asleep for nearly an hour now. Thomas Allen decides that it is safe to leave their shack and make the hike into town. When Thomas Allen finally arrives, the town is dark and the streets are empty, as it usually is during this time of the night. He goes straight to the bookstore and makes his way around to the back of the building. He then pushes open the window and climbs inside. "There it is...'And Then There Were None'," Thomas Allen says to himself, as he reads the title on the book's cover. Due to the fact that he's been reading since a very young age, Thomas Allen makes quick work of the 256 page novel. After finishing the novel, he returns it to the shelf from which he found it and then climbs back out of the window.

Suddenly, Thomas Allen hears someone shouting, "Stop right there! Don't you move, nigger!" the unknown voice demands. Thomas Allen doesn't move a muscle, he is completely motionless. "Put your hands against the wall," he hears someone say. Again, Thomas Allen does as he is told and places his hands against the wall. Then out of nowhere, Thomas Allen feels a throbbing sensation radiating from the back of his head. As he turns around to find out what's going on, a hard fist crashes against his cheek. Thomas Allen has never been in a fight, but it doesn't take much to realize that the three men in front of him are trying to do him harm. He tightly closes his giant hand into a fist and violently slings it forward. Like a brick flying through the air, his fist crashes against the chin of one of the men. For a brief moment, Thomas Allen sees the man's eyes staring at him in disbelief. And then his eyes roll backwards into his head as his body falls limp to the ground.

"I don't want to hurt you!" Thomas Allen shouts to the other two men.

Standing there motionless, in shock, one of them finally says, "Don't I know you?" Thomas Allen shakes his head to disagree. "Yes I do. You're that white nigger, Thomas something." At that moment, Thomas Allen recognizes the man's face. But, he's not a man at all, in fact, he's Thomas Anthony, the school boy that Thomas Allen ran into years ago. But, his name is actually Henry Oliver. Thomas Allen then tries to leave.

"Hey! Where you think you're going?" Henry says.

"I ain't looking for any trouble, just let me be on my way," Thomas Allen replies.

"We're getting the law," Henry says, as he and the other boy make a break for the sheriff's house. Thomas Allen sees this as an opportunity to get away and quickly sprints towards the woods.

As he arrives back at the shack, he enters the door and immediately starts shouting for Elijah.

"Papa! Papa, wake up!"

Startled, Elijah jumps out of bed and stands in front of his son, who is now bent over at the waist trying to catch his breath.

"What's wrong?" Elijah asks.

Thomas Allen then explains the entire situation to his father. Although, highly disgusted and in total disbelief of what his son just told him, Elijah knows what he must now do in order to protect his son.

Nearly a week has passed since Thomas Allen's run in with Henry Oliver and his two friends. Elijah prepares to head into town and demands that Thomas Allen stay behind.

"If they find you, they gonna kill you," Elijah says, to drive a sense of urgency into his son. Thomas Allen lowers his head and slowly nods, in agreement. Elijah then loads the old, makeshift wagon with four chickens, two baskets of eggs, three bottles of fresh goat's milk and four large bundles of chopped wood. As he lifts the handles of the wagon, Elijah can hear the wood crack due to the pressure of the heavy load. And then very slowly, he pulls the wagon to town.

It takes Elijah seven grueling hours to reach the trade post.

"Elroy," Elijah says, as he tilts his head forward, in a nodding gesture of hello.

"Elijah," Elroy replies, as he returns the nodding gesture.

"Need your help," Elijah says.

"I heard your boy got some trouble."

"He do," Elijah replies, before letting out a deep sigh.

"How your boy holdin' up?"

"He scared, says he killed one of them."

Elroy releases his thunderish laugh. "No...no...he jus' breaked him up real good. I heard he broke da boys jaw, in three places," Elroy replies.

"That's good to hear."

Elroy softly shakes his head as though he disagrees.

"What?" Elijah asks.

"Dat boy...is da judge son. He ain't too happy bout negroes bustin' up whites in his town. Hell, he got half da town looking for your boy, Elijah."

"That's why I need your help. This is all the supplies I could spare. I'll bring more later, my word."

"No," Elroy replies, with his deep voice sounding like the roar of a lion.

Elijah doesn't reply, he simply just stares at the dirt beneath his bare feet.

"I ain't taking your things. We needs to stick together in times like dese," Elroy says.

"What do I need to do?" Elijah asks.

"You needs to get dat boy way from here."

"How am I supposed to do that?" Elijah replies, as he shrugs his shoulders and tilts his hands in the air. "Past few days da army been walking the street lookin' for new recruits. They say a big war jus started They need all da hands they can get."

"Thomas Allen ain't old enough for no army business...he ain't but 16."

"It be the easiest way to get him out of here. Imma get papers made dat say he 18."

"Then what?" Elijah replies.

"I heard one of them army boys say dat they was comin' back dis Saturday. So, way I figure...you just make sure your boy here when they is and ill take care of da rest."

Elijah makes the grueling trip back home through the thick woods of Mississippi. Upon his arrival, Thomas Allen is waiting for him on the porch.

"You get the chores done?" Elijah asks.

"Yes sir."

"Good. Son, we need to talk, but I need to get cleaned up first."

Thomas Allen nods his head. Elijah gets cleaned up and then eats a leftover biscuit and a few pieces of bacon. After finishing his supper, he makes his way back to the porch where Thomas Allen is still patiently waiting.

"Is he dead, Papa?" Thomas Allen asks, as Elijah sits down on the porch.

Elijah shakes his head and says, "Naw...he ain't dead...just broke his jaw."

"That's good, right?" Thomas Allen replies.

Elijah takes a deep breath and then slowly lets it out, "Son, whites don't like when we hurt one of their kind. You're gonna have to go away for awhile."

"Go away? Where?"

"The army... it'll be good for you, son."

"What about you? What are you going to do, Papa?" Thomas Allen replies, as he feels a slight burning sensation in his nose and his eyes began to water.

"I'll be fine...ain't no one looking for me. Yous the one they want."

"Yes sir," Thomas Allen replies, as his eyes are no longer able to contain the tears that have been building up.

"Elroy taking care of things, you'll be leaving out Saturday."

"No...that's only three days, Papa."

"It's already done. You going Saturday and that's the end of it," Elijah says, as he stands up and walks towards the chicken coop.

He can't let Thomas Allen see his pain. He must stay strong in his son's eyes, so that his son will grow into a strong man. But the truth is, he will miss his boy dearly.

Chapter 6

The three days have passed and it is now early Saturday morning. Elijah and Thomas Allen make the hike into town together. The walk through the woods only takes four hours without pulling the weight of the wagon behind them. Shortly after 9 a.m., they arrive at Elroy's trade post.

"Elroy," Elijah says, as he nods his head.

"I gots da papers...hide da boy inside," Elroy replies.

Thomas Allen slowly opens the small wooden door located behind Elroy. The old rusted hinges, which look to be fairly supporting the weight of the door, let out an eerie squeak as the door opens. As he closes the door behind him, the hinges squeak once again. The high pitched noise makes Thomas Allen's skin crawl. In fact, his skin is now covered with tiny bumps. Inside the little shack there is one cot, a metal bucket used for washing, a table, a wooden chair and an old railroad lantern. The lantern provides a dim glow throughout the tiny shack. Thomas Allen sits in the chair and waits.

Outside Elroy hands the papers to Elijah.

"Thank you," Elijah says, as he takes the papers from Elroy's hand.

Elroy shakes his head and replies, "Nevermind."

"Now what?" Elijah asks.

"Now we wait til' we sees dat army boy. Then we call him over and tell him we gots somebody he needs to meet."

Elijah doesn't reply with words he simply Just nods his head and waits.

It's nearly two hours later when the army boy and two dozen fresh recruits roll into town.

"Dats him right there," Elroy says, as he points to a white boy wearing a soldier's uniform.

The boy looks to be about 19 years old. He's tall, but not quite as tall as Thomas Allen and not nearly as filled out with muscles. But, there's something about the way the boy carries himself that tells Elijah, he's not someone that should be messed with. Elijah motions the boy to come over, by fanning his hands in the air towards himself. The boy makes a fist and holds it in the air with his elbow making a perfect 90 degree angle. Then immediately everyone behind him stops at once.

The boy walks over and says, "You look a little old for the army."

"No sir, it's not for me. It's my boy," Elijah replies.

"And how old is your boy?" the young soldier asks.

"He 18, got his papers right here," Elroy says, as he waves the papers in the air.

The soldier nods his head takes a breath and then looks back at his recruits, as if he were evaluating them.   "Alright, I could use one more. Where is he now?" the soldier says.

"Thomas Allen, come out here," Elijah says.

Almost immediately after, the door slowly opens letting out yet another high pitched squeak.

"Yes sir," Thomas Allen says, as he steps out of the shack.

"This is my boy. He's 18 now, so I guess he's the man," Elijah says, as he points towards Thomas Allen.

Thomas Allen knows that he's not 18, but he also knows that if his father says something, he has reasons. The soldier moves closer to Thomas Allen and says, "Do you want to fight for your country?"

"I never want to fight, but I will if I have to."

"You speak like you have been educated well," the soldier replies. The soldier then grabs a hold of Thomas Allen, to feel the strength of his muscles. He then takes a step back and says, "I'm Lieutenant Long and you'll do just fine. Private Ryan, bring me an enlistment form." Private Ryan, which is another young white soldier, comes marching over with a form in his hand. Lieutenant Long takes the paper and asks, "Can you write your name?"

"Yes sir, I can."

"Good, put it right here, Lieutenant Long says, as he points at a dotted line on the paper.

Thomas Allen puts his name on the line and hands the paper back to Lieutenant Long.

"Get in line with the rest of them and do whatever the man in front of you does," Lieutenant Long demands.

Thomas Allen does as he is told. And then the group begins marching out of town.

Just before reaching the end of town the group suddenly stops, there's someone else that wants to join. After ten minutes, a white boy gets in line right next to Thomas Allen.

"You," the boy whispers to Thomas Allen. Thomas Allen looks at the white boy and smiles before saying, "Looks like your the white nigger now, yous in da back of da line wit rest of us."

Thomas Allen purposely made himself sound less educated as though to mock Henry Oliver.

"It better not be no talking in my line! Now move out!" Lieutenant Long shouts.

The group marches on and neither Thomas Allen nor Henry Oliver speak another word to one another. They marched to a mobilized training facility, which would later be known as Keesler Field. There, the recruits from all over the area were given supplies, weapons and very limited training. The army simply couldn't train raw recruits fast enough to keep up with the war overseas. After an extremely short two weeks, Thomas Allen and the rest of the recruits were divided up and sent to war.

Chapter 7

Lieutenant Long hand selected
Thomas Allen, Private Ryan, and Henry
Oliver along with 30 other qualified recruits
to be in his regiment.

Now six months later, Lieutenant
Long's regiment is roaming throughout
Poland on strict orders to seek and destroy,
which basically means seek out the enemy
and destroy them. After six months of
surviving and killing together, Thomas Allen
and Henry Oliver no longer look at each
other the way that they once did. In the
midst of war there's no longer a line dividing
blacks and whites. Instead, that line has been
replaced with us or them meaning allies or
the enemy.

At the young age of 16, Thomas Allen
has seen things that no man should ever be
forced to see. Every day is full of bloodshed,
tears and the fear of never returning home.

But, through all the chaos surrounding them and regardless of their past history, a friendship has begun to blossom between Thomas Allen and Henry Oliver.

April 5, 1942, American soldiers have been in the war for nearly a year now. Lieutenant Long's regiment along with Thomas Allen and 'Olly', as Henry Oliver is called now, have just come across a major Nazi execution camp. The camp is located in the Poland territory, right outside of Chelmno. The regiment has witnessed plenty of war action and have seen many people die over the past year. But, none of them were prepared to see a German Nazi execution camp.

Hidden by the cover of the night, the regiment slowly approaches the heavily gated camp. By this time of the war, they have all heard stories of these camps but, none of them have seen one first hand.

"Olly, there's a boy by the fence," Thomas Allen whispers.

Olly nods, as though to say he sees him as well and then places his left index finger over his lips, as a gesture of silence.

Thomas Allen turns his wrist to face the palms of his hands to the sky and whispers, "We can't just leave him here."

The truth of the matter is they've seen wild dogs on the trails that were better nourished than the boy. As Thomas Allen moves closer to the fence, the boy cowers down into the fetal position. Though only a light dusting of moonlight shines on the boys shirtless body, Thomas Allen can see every bone beneath the boys skin.

"I ain't gonna hurt you. We're the good guys," Thomas Allen says to the boy.

The boy is filthy. The horrific odor coming from his body can be smelled from the other side of the fence.

"Hey, leave that boy alone. Look!" Olly says, as he points deeper into the camp. "There's armed enemy soldiers patrolling the camp."

"Move out," Lieutenant Long says.

Thomas Allen pulls a chocolate bar from his pocket and sticks it in the fence as he says, "Here, eat this." He then retreats with the rest of his regiment. There is currently only seventeen men in the regiment. Many have died and some have transferred to other outfits. In the safety of a patch of woods, near to the camp, Lieutenant Long orders the men to dig in for the night.

Thomas Allen couldn't sleep that

night. Every time he closed his eyes, vivid images of the boy's bones poking out of his skin clouded his mind. He began wondering how a boy that couldn't be any more than five years old, could possibly live through something like this. He suddenly realized that his home in Mississippi didn't seem so bad after all.

"Olly, you still awake?" Thomas Allen says.

"Yeah."

"We have to save that boy, Olly."

"I heard they have hundreds of people in these camps. We can't risk the lives of all of them, just to save one boy. Lieutenant Long called for reinforcements," Olly says.

"Reinforcements?" Thomas Allen replies with confusion in his voice.

"Yeah, they're sending three regiments, so that we can take the camp."

"When?" Thomas Allen replies.

"I think I heard them say it will take three days."

"Three days? They could all be dead by then."

"We have our orders, the only thing we can do is wait. Now get some sleep, Thomas Allen," Olly replies.

Later that night, Thomas Allen finally

falls asleep. Thomas Allen usually doesn't dream at night, but this is anything other than the usual night. He dreams of saving the boy from the camp. He doesn't know exactly how, but one way or the other the boy and he are back at his father's shack in Mississippi. The boy is clean and well nourished with his bright blue eyes now happily capturing rays from the glimmering summer sun. Although the boy doesn't speak in the dream, Thomas Allen can feel the sense of appreciation from the boy.

Suddenly the sounds of gunshots and screams fill the cold morning air. Thomas Allen is now awake and so is the rest of his regiment. As they move to the edge of the woods and glance at the camp, they can now see thousands of refugees, not hundreds, as the gunshots continue and the screams grow louder. The refugees are shouting, but the regiment's translator was killed two days ago, so no one knows what they're saying.

But fear is a universal language and these people are scared to death. No, they're scared of death.

"They're killing them all!" Thomas Allen shouts, as he stares at his Lieutenant.

"We have orders," Lieutenant Long replies.

"We can't just let them die," Thomas Allen says.

"Stand down soldier! We have our orders!" Lieutenant Long replies.

It was still the early morning hours, where the sun had just began to peek, but still yet to rise. In the cover of what darkness still remains, Thomas Allen makes his move.

"I wont let this happen!" he shouts as he makes a break for the far back corner of the camp. Olly and four others quickly follow. The six men gather at the back fence line.

"We're with you, Thomas Allen," Olly says.

Thomas Allen nods as to thank them.

"I counted ten men doing the shooting and five more moving the bodies," Thomas Alan says.

"Do you have a plan?" Olly asks.

Thomas Allen smiles and replies, "Save the people."

"I got a small pair of wire cutters," one of the other men says, as he pulls them from a small pouch that he's carrying.

Thomas Allen cut the fence and then crawls through the hole, belly down. After all six men have made it through the hole, they gather once again behind a small wooden structure.

"Tex and Olly, you're with me." Tex is a 20 year old negro from Arkansas. He's not very big but, overall, he's proven to be a good soldier. "We're taking out the shooters," Thomas Allen says.

Olly and Tex nod their heads to confirm.

"You three go around the back and take out the body stackers, before they have a chance to reach their weapons," Thomas Allen says, as he points at the other three men.

"Everyone watch your back, we don't know how many more there are of them," Olly says.

"On my signal, we will go," Thomas Allen says.

The other three men move down the back fence line, staying hidden in the rapidly fading darkness. Thomas Allen waits until the men are in position and then he gives the signal. Thomas Allen, Olly and Tex run out of the shadows and into the bright morning. The other three men do the same. Thomas Allen shows no fear, nor hesitation, as he rushes towards the ten enemy gunman. He points his weapon and continuously squeezes the trigger. Thomas Allen has already dropped four men, neither Olly or Tex clear a single shot. The five men that was stacking the bodies hear the gunshots and scramble for their weapons, but they never get the chance, caught off guard and unarmed they're quickly disposed of. Olly and Tex shoot three more of the gunman. The remaining three drop their weapons and quickly throw their hands above their heads.

"Are there any more?" Thomas Allen shouts, as he shoves the barrel of his gun in one of the surrendering enemy's face.

The man starts spouting out gibberish in German.

"1...2...3," Thomas Allen slowly counts as he points at the remaining enemy soldiers, and then repeats, "Are there any more," as he waves his hand around the camp.

"Nicht, nicht, nicht," the man replies, as he franticly shakes his head.

"Est ist nicht mehr," one of the other men says.   During the gunfire, the remaining refugees dropped to the ground for cover. With a strong Polish accent, one of them slowly stands and says, "He say there is no more."

"You speak English?" Thomas Allen says.

The tiny old woman can barely stand,

but somehow musters the strength to nod and say, "Yes."

"Here, sit down," Olly says, as he helps the woman to the ground.

"I'm looking for a boy that was by the fence last night," Thomas Allen says, to the old woman.

As she begins to cry, she looks over her left shoulder at the stack of bodies.

"Ivan...grandson," she says.

"He is your grandson?"

The woman slowly shakes her head no, "He was...they kill him."

"I'm sorry," Thomas Allen says, as he holds the woman's hand.

"NA...NA...NA," she mutters, "He tell me chocolate man give him chocolate. He say you, chocolate man, save us. He say you good guys," the woman says, as she smiles exposing her toothless gums.

Tears began to roll from Thomas Allen's eyes as he hears the news of the innocent child's death. By now the crowd of refugees are all standing or struggling to stand. Shortly after, Lieutenant Long and the rest of the regiment have broken through the front fence and joined the six heroes. When suddenly, Tex collapses, he's been shot. And from the looks of his wound he won't live through the night.

They did everything that they could to save Tex's life that night, but when it was all said and done the 20 year old boy, from Arkansas, slips away. Although Thomas Allen doesn't feel the pressure of black and white anymore, it was nice not being the only one around. Time passes on, the war continues and so does the killing and dying. By the end of the war in 1945, an estimated 400 thousand plus American soldiers have died. Olly, Lieutenant Long, Thomas Allen and two of the six heroes from that day all survive the war. Thomas Allen left Mississippi a 16 year old boy, but returned a 20 year old war hero, whose actions saved hundreds of lives.

Chapter 8

Six months after the war was over, Thomas Allen got word that his friend Olly was receiving an award. It's funny how, when it came to life and death, Olly didn't hesitate to stand with Thomas Allen. But the minute their feet touched Mississippi, Olly was no longer Olly, he was Henry Oliver. Although he no longer mistreats Thomas Allen, he won't exactly admit friendship either. Either way, Thomas Allen is glad to hear that Olly will be recognized for his duties.

Thomas Allen quickly realizes that not many things in Mississippi have changed, over the time that he was gone. It seems that blacks have the right to fight for their country, but yet they don't have the right to go to the same school, eat in the same restaurants or even share the same sidewalks with whites. *Painted by prejudice,* Thomas Allen thinks to himself. He now understands what his father meant all those years ago.

It turns out that Henry Oliver is being recognized as quite the war hero. The army is giving him the congressional medal of honor. Lieutenant Long says that on April 5, 1942, himself, Olly and four other white soldiers raided a large Nazi execution camp. And by doing so, they saved the lives of thousands of refugees. Only three of the men receiving the medal of honor were actually part of the raid that day. Lieutenant Long claims that Henry Oliver showed great poise and easily took control of the situation, leading the six men to victory over 25 enemy soldiers. Thomas Allen doesn't care about the medal or who does or doesn't get it. But it hurts him that Olly and the other two men, that were actually there with him that day, would willingly stand next to these men as they accept the medals and recognition for something that they had no part of. And it burns him to think that Tex died doing what these men claim to have done.

A few years have passed since the end of the war. By the early 1950s, major movements started taking form. African Americans all over the states had begun to make a stand. Some would simply refuse to be treated less than equal, while others peacefully protested and fought for equality.

In 1954, The US Supreme Court ruled that schools in all states were to be integrated. This was a major piece of history that would eventually pave the way for complete desegregation. It sent a message to the black community, that however slow it may be, change is on the way. A year later, in Montgomery, Alabama, an event took place that would spark a nation and set fire to the entire African American community. In 1955, Rosa Parks boarded a public bus and took a seat near the front. When asked to move and take her proper seat near the back, she politely refused. The bus was ultimately grounded and the police were called to escort Miss Parks off of the bus. One woman's courage to stand and fight for what she believed in, would give courage to thousands more.

The year is now 1960. Henry Oliver has accepted a job in Washington, DC with the. United States army. Although, Thomas Allen hasn't spoken with Olly since returning from the war in 1949, he still thinks about his old friend from time to time. Now at the age of 36, Thomas Allen is attending a small biblical college in Alabama, where he can fully learn and understand the true meaning of his favorite childhood book the "oly ible" or to be correct the Holy Bible. Thomas Allen sits at one of the coloreds tables in his school's cafeteria. When suddenly, one of his black classmates comes running up to him.

"Did you hear?" the classmate asks.

"Did I hear what, Anthony?" Thomas Allen replies, as he slightly rolls his eyes upwards to make contact with Anthony's.

"About the four black students in North Carolina." Thomas Allen shakes his head as to imply that he had not heard about this.

"They sat at the whites only table in their school cafeteria." Thomas Allen shrugs his shoulders. "That's not the best part. The white waitress wouldn't take their order, so they refused to leave. They sat there all day, until it closed," Anthony says.

Up until now, Thomas Allen didn't pay much attention to the movement. But when he heard the news of four brave college students, his eyes widened and he began to think.

"That's good...it's time for change," Thomas Allen replies.

The news quickly spread about the four college students. All over the nation, groups of African Americans were organizing sit-ins at whites only restaurants. Thomas Allen and Anthony have also organized one of these sit-ins in a whites-only restaurant near the campus of their school. Thomas Allen, Anthony and three of their friends enter a whites-only restaurant and quietly take seats at an empty table. The restaurant named Anne's Kitchen, is relatively empty on this particular day. The cook, an older white woman, whom Thomas Allen assumed was Anne, a young white waitress with blonde hair and blue eyes and three middle-aged white men sitting at the counter, were all that were in the restaurant. As they take their seats, Thomas Allen notices that the waitress whispers something to the three men.

"You niggers ain't supposed to be in here," one of the men says, as he twists his butt on the bar stool so that he is now facing in the direction of the table. Thomas Allen, Anthony, nor any of the others say a word.

"Did you hear me boy's? We ain't gonna have this nonsense around here!" the man shouts.

But once again Thomas Allen and his group of friends remain silent. Thomas Allen notices that the men are now talking quietly amongst themselves. Then one of them stands up and exits the restaurant as he shakes his head in disbelief. Moments later, the man returns with a small group of ten white males, ranging in age from 16 to their early twenties.

"Now you boys get up and go home and there ain't got to be no trouble," one of the men still sitting at the counter says.

It never ceases to amaze Thomas Allen, how someone with such freedom to learn can still manage to murder the English Language. But still, Thomas Allen and his group remain silent. The man makes eye contact with the cook, through the order window. The older woman then nods her head.

"Alright boys, let's do this," the man at the counter says to the other white men. The 13 white men began gathering trash cans full of food scraps along with other spoiled trash, buckets of water and a bag of flour. "Last chance," one of the white men shouts. Still no response from Thomas Allen or his group. The white man began dumping the trash and food scraps over the top of each member of the group's head. The smell is foul, but nothing like the boy that Thomas Allen saw during the war. The white men then dump the buckets of water on each of the men in Thomas Allen's group. The white men then follow the buckets of water by dumping flour over Thomas Allen and his friends.

"Y'all wanted to be white, well there you go," one of the younger white men says.

As Thomas Allen looks across the table at Anthony, now covered in flour, he's immediately reminded of the day his father looked like this as well. He then begins to laugh.

"You think this is funny?" the young white man says, as he punches Thomas Allen in the back of the head.

Thomas Allen stands up and towers over the man. With his massive arms, that look more like tree branches, hanging by his sides, Thomas Allen looks at the man and says, "One day, you will remember my mercy, strength and courage for you have just been painted by my prejudice.. May God be with you during your struggles, as though I know he is here with me during mine. Ill pray for your tainted soul. So that God may give you the wisdom and knowledge that your heart so desperately needs." And then Thomas Allen, followed by the rest of his group, peacefully exits the restaurant. Thomas Allen doesn't know if it was his intimidating stature or his words that put the fear in that man's eyes, but whatever it was, he was glad for it.

In 1963, Thomas Allen joined a group of over 250,000 nonviolent protestors. The protesters marched through Washington, DC, on their way to the Lincoln Memorial. Dr. Martin Luther King, Jr. led the march and that was also where he gave his famous, "I have a dream" speech. The march was aimed to gain the government's awareness of the Civil Rights Bill.

In 1965, Thomas Allen joined Dr. Martin Luther King, Jr. and nearly 30,000 white and black Americans for yet another march. This march went from Salem to Montgomery, Alabama. The march was focused on the unfairness of blacks having to pay a tax to vote and how many African Americans were being harassed while trying to vote. The march proved to be a success, later that year, the Voting Rights Act was passed. All the laws that once kept blacks and whites segregated in America had now been abolished. The American people, blacks and whites alike, were now truly one nation under God.

It is now 1972, Thomas Allen has just

received the word that his father has passed away. Thomas Allen returns to Mississippi to attend Elijah's burial services. After the funeral, Thomas Allen is approached by a man that claims to be Elijah's attorney.

"My name is William P. Harris, I need to speak with you about your father's will," the man says.

Thomas Allen had no idea that his father had a written will, much less an attorney. Thomas Allen nods his head.

"Come by my office later today, it's located right here in town," the man says, as he hands Thomas Allen a business card with the office's address printed on it.

Again, Thomas Allen nods his head as he places the card in his pocket.

Later that afternoon, Thomas Allen decides to stop by and see what this attorney has to say.

"Come in, come in," Mr. Harris says, as Thomas Allen enters the door. Thomas Allen politely takes a seat on the opposite side of Mr Harris. With nothing but a beautiful, large, cherry wood desk between them, Mr. Harris says, "I was truly hoping you would stop by. Your father was very proud of you, Thomas Allen."

"Thank you."

"I guess you are ready to know why I've asked you here today," Mr Harris says.

"Yes sir...I am."

"I have the deed to your father's property...," Mr Harris begins to say before Thomas Allen interrupts. "My father's property? He never actually owned that property."

Mr Harris smiles and then replies, "He officially purchased the property several years ago. And two years ago, when his health started to worsen, he came to me and asked if I would make a written will, naming you the sole heir of his property."

Thomas Allen doesn't know how to react. All of this is a shock to him, his father had never told him of any of it.

"Alright, so what now?" Thomas Allen asks.

"Just the formalities...all I need is for you to sign some paperwork."

Thomas Allen then sign the paperwork and in return Mr Harris gives him the property deed. Thomas Allen is now the proud owner of the land of which he grew up on. When Thomas Allen arrives back at his childhood home, the shack is still the shack. But, due to his father's health the land no longer looks maintained at all and the animals are now all gone. *If I'm going to live here, then I'll have to find a job,* Thomas Allen thinks to himself.

The next morning, Thomas Allen returns back to town, which by car no longer takes hours. After asking several of the business owners in town if they are in need of help, Thomas Allen finally comes across a man that just might be able to help him in his search of work.

"I heard the local church might be looking for someone to help out," the man tells Thomas Allen.

The man looks to be well into his 60's or early 70's. Suddenly it hits him, Thomas Allen realizes that he knows this man.

"Elroy? Is that you?" Thomas Allen asks.

The man begins to laugh. Although his old lungs are no longer full of thunderous laughter, Thomas Allen can tell that this man is indeed Elroy.

"Your father told me you was going ta school ta be a preacher," Elroy says.

"Yes sir...I did."

"Is Dat right? Well, Go on down to da church. Ask for Benny, tell him who you is and that I sent you," Elroy replies, as he points down the street, towards the church.

"Yes sir, thank you."

Thomas Allen makes his way to the church and does as Elroy told him.

"You Elijah's boy? I've been waiting on you," Benny says.

"You knew my father?"

"I knew him very well. He was a fine member of this church and he told me all about you."

"Elroy told me that you might need some help around the church."

Benny begins to laugh, "Is that what he told you?" he says, through his laughter.

"Yes sir."

"I don't need help son. I need someone to take my place as the pastor."

Thomas Allen thinks about the situation before replying, "I don't have any experience of running my own church."

"Nonsense! Your father told me about your schooling and I believe you will do just fine," Benny replies.

And with that said, Thomas Allen just became the pastor at the New Light Church of Christ.

By 1975, Thomas Allen has fully settled into his role as the pastor of his very own church. Although, Benny was a wonderful teacher and Thomas Allen learned quickly, it wasn't always easy. In fact, sometimes it was downright hard. Preparing sermons send a morning and afternoon, the Wednesday night sermons, the youth groups and of course the charity fundraisers. And with all of this already on his plate, he still has to manage his time to find ways to meet individually with members of the church. They all have their problems and issues, some with bills while others are in need of marital counseling. But, not one is too big or small for Thomas Allen to give his time.

Now that Thomas Allen fully understands the Bible and most of its hidden messages, he also now understands that it creates a bridge between himself and God. One can decide to cross the bridge and be joined with God on the other side, or you can simply refuse the path laid out before you and go in search of your own route. But, whichever way one decides to go, all roads will eventually lead to the same place. Regardless of the path you may choose, one day we will all be standing on the other side of that bridge next to God where he will pass his judgment upon us. Thomas Allen spoke these words during his first sermon as pastor of the New Light Church of Christ. Now three years later, he is still spreading

God's words and drawing more and more
souls to the bridge that directly leads to God.

Chapter 9

By 1991, word within the religious communities had spread across the nation about a pastor from Mississippi and his unique approach of telling God's Word. By the end of the year, Thomas Allen had traveled to several different states, spreading the word with him like a wildfire on a dry windy day.

By 1995, Thomas Allen had been approached by hundreds of reverends, pastors and preachers. All of which, just wanted him to take part in their revivals. Although, he obviously didn't have time to take part in all of them, he did the very best that he could.

Over the years since the war, Thomas Allen hasn't really thought much of it. But, on January 13, 1997 that would change. Not one Congressional Medal of Honor was awarded to a black soldier from WWII. In 1993, the army conducted an investigation which would later prove that several different men deserved the honor. On January 13, 1997, President Bill Clinton awarded 7 African American soldiers with the Medal of Honor. Although, thrilled for the men receiving the award, it made Thomas Allen think of that awful day in Poland, and the little boy Ivan. But as quickly as the thoughts came, they passed.

By 2012, Thomas Allen has traveled all over the world. And together, with God, he has helped save thousands of souls. He is, by no means, a perfect man, there was only one of those. But his love for mankind is strong and his faith in God is even stronger. Thomas Allen believes that it was his faith that brought a familiar face through the doors of his church.

"Olly?" Thomas Allen says, as an old white man, being pushed in a wheelchair buy a younger man in his mid 30's, enters the church.

The old man shakes his head to acknowledge that he is in fact Olly. The younger man then leaves them to talk alone.

"Hello, Thomas Allen."

"Good to see you, Olly."

"That's my great grandson," Olly says, as he points towards the door.

"He looks just like you once did."

Both men laugh a little.

"What brings you by after all these years?" Thomas Allen asks.

"I heard of a pastor from Mississippi that has been saving souls everywhere he goes. And then I heard his name. So, I had to come see it with my own eyes, while I still can," Olly replies.

"I'm glad you did. I thought about you from time to time, over the years," Thomas Allen says.

Olly slowly nods his head as he begins to sob heavily.

"Its alright," Thomas Allen says, as he places his hands over Olly's.

"No..no it's not," Olly says, as he forces the words over his trembling lips. "I brought something for you," Olly says, as he begins to gain control of his emotions. He reaches in his coat pocket and pulls something out, then places it in Thomas Allen's hand as he says, "For Ivan, he would want you to have it." Thomas Allen's eyes, that have seen the world at its best and worst, begin to fill with tears as he looks at the object in his hand. It's the Congressional Medal of Honor. Both men cry as they share their memories of that day. Olly told Thomas Allen of how all the other men that received the Medal of Honor that day had passed away. That he was the only one still alive, that knew the truth. He told Thomas Allen that he would be willing to report the truth to the officials. But, Thomas Allen declined. The fact that Olly, instead of Henry Oliver, showed up in his church meant more to him than recognition. After all, God was there that day and he knows the truth. That's good enough for Thomas Allen.

Two weeks later, Thomas Allen received a phone call from Henry Oliver's great grandson. It seems that Olly's health had been failing him for many years. And after making good on some of the wrong that he had done, he was finally able to let go and rest peacefully.

I met Thomas Allen, for the first time, a year later in 2013. We quickly became friends and he would tell me stories about his life and dreams. It truly hurt Thomas Allen to see today's generation wasting what he, and so many others, fought so hard for. He never could understand why people that have the right to dream and chase those dreams, never slow down to appreciate them. He truly felt that this generation of Americans, not just black or white but all Americans, have become lazy and too dependent on technology. He asked me to tell his story, so that people would know how hard it was to continue fighting. The sad thing is...is that his story was just one of many more. The last thing Thomas Allen ever said to me was, "We all have trials and tribulations. But yet, it's how we handle them and what we choose to do afterward that makes us who we truly are."

Thomas Allen quietly and gently passed away on January 1, 2014, at the age of 88. Nearly 1,500 people, from all walks of life, attended his burial service. Many of them were people that he had met during his revivals or someone he had stopped on the street to say a friendly 'hello.' Thomas Allen was loved and will be missed by many. Sometimes it makes me wonder how a man that started his life with so little, left it with everything. I can only hope that by writing this book, that I have given Thomas Allen a voice beyond his death. If only one person that reads this book begins to make better decisions and gain control of their life as Thomas Allen did. Then his story and work will forever live on, Amen. He was a true man of color, war and faith. Therefore, his story deserves to be loved and shared by many.

The End

Special Thanks

We would like to thank the great people of our Country's past, the ones whom actually had to live and survive those horrible times. May God be forever in your favor, thank you for paving the way to a brighter future.

Disclaimer

This book was based on actual events, but names, places and some events were fabricated for the storyline.